THE ART OF SELF MANAGEMENT

A Great Way to Build Good Habits, Acquire Knowledge and Skills, Develop Growth Mindset, and Become The Updated Version Of Yourself.

PRADIP DAS

© Copyright 2024 - All rights reserved.

The content contained within this book may not be reproduced, duplicated, or transmitted without direct written permission from the author or the publisher. Under no circumstances will any blame or legal responsibility be held against the publisher, or author, for any damages, reparation, or monetary loss due to the information contained within this book. Either directly or indirectly.

Legal Notice:

This book is copyright protected. This book is only for personal use. You cannot amend, distribute, sell, use, quote or paraphrase any part, or the content within this book, without the consent of the author or publisher.

Disclaimer Notice:

Please note the information contained within this document is for educational and entertainment purposes only. All effort has been executed to present accurate, up to date, and reliable, complete information. No warranties of any kind are declared or implied. Readers acknowledge that the author is not engaging in the rendering of legal, financial, medical or professional advice. The content within this book has been derived from various sources. Please consult a licensed professional before attempting any techniques outlined in this book.

By reading this document, the reader agrees that under no circumstances is the author responsible for any losses, direct or indirect, which are incurred as a result of the use of information contained within this document, including, but not limited to, — errors, omissions, or inaccuracies.

Author Profile

Table of Contents

Table of Contents 4
Introduction 5
Self-reflection and Awareness 13
Identifying Strengths and Weaknesses.............. 17
Develop Growth Mindset.................................. 22
Build Good Habits... 26
Build Self-discipline... 29
Stress Management.. 34
Time Management 38
Emotional Intelligence 43
Decision Making 47
Continuous Learning... 51
Communication Skills.. 55
Adaptability.. 58
Accountability... 62
Sense of Purpose 66
Motivation.. 69
Resilience 72
Conclusion.. 75
Self-Management Checklist 77

Introduction

Ever wondered how some individuals seamlessly face the complexities of life, achieving their goals with finesse and resilience? What if I revealed that the key to their success lies in mastering the art of self-management? Imagine the disciplined routines of visionary leaders who turned startups into global empires. Visualize the meticulous planning of athletes who transformed challenges into victories on the global stages. These stories are not just narratives; they are living proof that the principles of self-management can drive you toward your aspirations, regardless of the field you choose to conquer.

Self-management is not just a skill; it's an art form—a dynamic interplay of understanding oneself, setting meaningful goals, and navigating the ever-changing landscape of emotions, challenges, and opportunities.

In this book, you will discover the deep impact of self-awareness, the strategic way of goal-setting, and the artistry of time management. From decision-making to continuous learning, from communication skills to resilience, each chapter explores a new layer of insight and actionable strategies.

This book is to encourage change with adaptability, and to develop accountability in every facet of your life. Whether you are a seasoned professional seeking personal mastery or an individual on the path of self-discovery, "The Art of Self-Management" provides a roadmap to not only steer but also prosper in the multifaceted journey of life.

So, get ready to be inspired, challenged, and transformed. The canvas is set, the stories are waiting to unfold, and the art of self-management signals you to get on a journey of self-discovery and achievement. Let the tales of triumph and the wisdom of successful individuals ignite your curiosity and fuel your own pursuit of excellence.

Understanding Self-Management:

At the heart of personal and professional success lies the core concept of self-management. It surpasses mere time management or organizational skills; it captures a holistic approach to connecting one's potential and navigating the complexities of life with intentionality. Self-management is not a rigid set of rules but rather an art form that adapts to individual aspirations, challenges, and environments.

Self-management involves the conscious and strategic allocation of resources—time, energy, and focus—to achieve specific objectives. It's about setting meaningful goals, understanding priorities, and aligning actions with long-term visions. The art of self-management empowers individuals to take charge of their lives that propels them towards personal and professional fulfillment.

The self-management requires a deep dive into one's own values, strengths, and aspirations. It demands introspection and an honest evaluation of one's current habits and routines. By understanding the principles of self-management, individuals gain the tools to develop discipline, resilience, and adaptability—key components in the pursuit of success.

The self-management explores the core principles that successful individuals across various domains have employed to achieve their goals. From establishing effective routines to cultivating a growth mindset, each aspect of self-management plays a pivotal role in shaping a fulfilling and purpose-driven life. So, let's embark on this journey of self-discovery and mastery.

Importance in Personal Development:

Raj was born into a small village family that could barely make ends meet, he faced the harsh realities of poverty and limited opportunities. Yet, amidst the adversity, he harbored a burning desire for something more—something that would defy the predetermined narrative of his circumstances.

Raj's journey took an unexpected turn when he stumbled upon a old book on personal development, discarded by someone who saw little value in its worn pages. Curiosity led Raj to explore the book's contents, and as he went into the principles of self-improvement, a spark ignited within him.

Fuelled by the transformative wisdom he found within those pages, Raj got on a relentless pursuit of education. He studied under the dim glow of a kerosene lamp, turning every challenge into an opportunity to prove to himself and the world that circumstances could be overcome.

As the years passed, Raj's dedication bore fruit. He crossed the complexities of his impoverished environment while immersing himself in personal development literature. Slowly, his mindset shifted, and he began to see possibilities where others saw limitations.

With firm determination, Raj aimed for the highest level of competitive exams—a feat unheard of in his village. The journey was grueling, marked by sleepless nights, sacrifice, and perseverance. Yet, with each passing day, Raj's confidence grew, fueled by the principles of self-improvement that had become his guiding light.

The day of the exam arrived, and Raj, armed with the knowledge he had acquired and the resilience he had cultivated, faced the daunting challenge. As the results were announced, the small village erupted in joy—Raj had not only cleared the exam but had secured a position among the top performers.

His success resonated far beyond the village borders, becoming an inspiration for others trapped in the clutches of poverty. Raj's story became an example of power of personal development, proving that with the right mindset, determination, and a thirst for knowledge, one could rise from the ashes of adversity to achieve greatness.

It is evident from the Raj's journey that personal development is not confined to the privileged; it is a beacon of hope that can illuminate even the darkest corners of life. Through his remarkable triumph, Raj dismantled the barriers of circumstance, proving that the pursuit of knowledge and personal growth knows no bounds.

The significance of self-management in personal development cannot be overstated. It serves as the foundational base upon which the structure of one's growth and progress is constructed. At its core, personal development is an ongoing journey of self-discovery, improvement, and the actualization of one's potential. Through effective self-management, individuals gain the ability to steer this journey consciously, aligning their actions with their aspirations.

A key aspect of personal development is the cultivation of self-awareness—a deep understanding of one's strengths, weaknesses, values, and aspirations. Self-management acts as the compass in this exploration, guiding individuals to navigate their internal landscapes and make intentional choices that propel them toward their goals. Without this compass, the path to personal development can be meandering and unclear.

Moreover, personal development often involves setting and achieving goals. Whether it's advancing in a career, adopting healthier habits, or pursuing lifelong dreams, self-management provides the tools to structure one's time, prioritize tasks, and maintain discipline. It's the force that transforms aspirations into concrete action plans, creating a roadmap for continuous improvement.

Self-management is the engine that drives personal development forward. It empowers individuals to take control of their destinies, developing resilience in the face of challenges and enabling adaptability to changing circumstances. As we delve deeper into the exploration of personal development in "The Art of Self-Management," the role of effective self-management will unfold as a foundation for unlocking one's true potential and realizing a life of purpose and fulfillment.

Self-reflection and Awareness

In our busy daily lives, where we are constantly juggling tasks and responsibilities, it's easy to lose sight of the most crucial element—ourselves. This is precisely where the magic of self-reflection and awareness comes into play. These tools are powerful instruments for self-management, offering guidance on the path to a more fulfilled and purposeful existence.

Understanding Self-Reflection: Imagine self-reflection as a pause button in the chaotic movie of life. It's that conscious moment where we step back to examine our thoughts, actions, and emotions. We ponder on why we react in certain ways and explore the underlying motivations behind our choices. Through self-reflection, we embark on a journey of understanding how our experiences shape our perspectives. It's like having a conversation with ourselves, unraveling the layers of our being to discover what makes us tick.

For instance, let's consider a scenario where a person consistently shies away from taking on leadership roles in a team. Through self-reflection, they might discover a deep-seated fear of failure or rejection, stemming from a childhood experience. Armed with this insight, they can consciously work towards overcoming this fear and accepting leadership opportunities, contributing to their personal and professional growth.

The Essence of Awareness: While self-reflection involves looking back, awareness is about being present in the moment. It's the art of observing ourselves without judgment, like a compassionate spectator of our own lives. Being aware means tuning in to our thoughts, emotions, and physical sensations. It's about acknowledging our strengths and weaknesses without criticism, understanding that these facets make us uniquely human.

Consider a hectic workday where stress levels are soaring. Someone practicing awareness might pause, take a few mindful breaths, and observe their feelings without being swept away by them.

This simple act of awareness can prevent impulsive reactions, developing a calm and composed response to challenges.

The true magic happens when self-reflection and awareness join forces. As we reflect on our past experiences, we become more aware of our behavioral patterns and tendencies. This heightened awareness becomes a guiding light, shaping our present actions and influencing our future choices.

Imagine a person who consistently finds themselves in unfulfilling relationships. Through self-reflection, they recognize patterns of seeking external validation due to a lack of self-worth. Armed with this awareness, they can consciously shift their approach to relationships, prioritizing self-love and attracting healthier connections.

In a world that often glorifies external achievements, the concept of looking inward might seem counterintuitive. However, self-reflection and awareness are not just personal indulgences; they are prerequisites for a meaningful life. Understanding ourselves on a deeper level is the foundation upon which we build resilience, forge authentic connections, and lead lives true to our values.

These tools offer a transformative journey, but it requires commitment. It's an investment in ourselves—a commitment to self-discovery that pays dividends in every aspect of our lives.

Therefore, let's not forget the vibrant thread that represents our own essence. Through self-reflection and awareness, we not only find ourselves but also create a life that resonates with authenticity, purpose, and deep fulfillment.

Identifying Strengths and Weaknesses

The journey of self-management and personal growth begins with a thorough exploration of our strengths and weaknesses. It's an exploration to discover the jewels that make us shine—the things we're good at—and identifying the areas where we have the potential to grow. It's a process of understanding ourselves better so that we can navigate life with more clarity and purpose.

The Power of Strengths:

Let's start with strengths – those special attributes that make each of us unique. Imagine you have a superpower, something you excel at effortlessly. Maybe it's the ability to solve complex problems, communicate with clarity, or ignite creativity in any situation. These are your strengths, the tools in your personal toolbox that can elevate your performance and enhance your overall well-being.

Sania, who discovered her strength in empathy, has an innate ability to understand and connect with others emotionally. She decided to channel this strength into a career in counseling, where her empathetic nature became a guiding light for those seeking support. By understanding her strength, Sania not only excelled in her chosen path but also found immense personal satisfaction.

Accepting Weaknesses as Opportunities:

Now, let's shift our focus to weaknesses. Instead of viewing them as stumbling blocks, think of weaknesses as untapped areas of potential growth. It takes courage to acknowledge these aspects of ourselves, but in doing so, we open the door to improvement and development.

Pritam realized a weakness in public speaking in himself. Rather than shying away from situations that required him to speak in front of others, he decided to confront this weakness head-on. Pritam enrolled in public speaking courses, sought guidance from experienced speakers, and gradually transformed this weakness into a skill. Today, he confidently addresses audiences, turning what was once a challenge into a triumph.

Aligning Actions with Values:

Self-management involves aligning our actions with our values and goals. Understanding our strengths allows us to direct towards activities and roles that resonate with our authentic selves. If problem-solving is your specialty, you might find fulfillment in roles that require innovative solutions. If creativity is a strength, you might pursue that avenue for personal satisfaction.

On the flip side, recognizing weaknesses enables us to make intentional choices. If time management is an area of improvement, developing strategies to organize and prioritize tasks becomes essential. If effective communication is identified as a weakness, investing time in communication workshops or seeking mentorship can be transformative.

Practical Tools for Identification:

To identify strengths and weaknesses, practical tools such as self-assessment quizzes, feedback from peers and mentors, and regular introspection can be immensely helpful.

Using a self-assessment tool can provide valuable insights into your preferences, values, and strengths. Receiving feedback from those around you offers a different perspective, helping you see aspects of yourself that might be overlooked. Regular reflection, perhaps through journaling, creates a space for ongoing self-discovery.

Utilizing Strengths and Addressing Weaknesses:

Once identified, the next step is utilizing strengths and addressing weaknesses. Suppose you discover a strength in strategic thinking. In that case, you might intentionally seek projects that require planning and foresight, allowing you to contribute your best. On the other hand, if a weakness in time management is recognized, creating a schedule, setting priorities, and employing time-management techniques become essential tools for improvement.

In nutshell, the process of identifying strengths and weaknesses is not about achieving perfection but about go on a continuous journey of self-improvement. Accepting both aspects contributes to a holistic understanding of oneself, cultivating resilience and adaptability in the face of life's uncertainties. It's like having a personal roadmap, guiding you towards a purposeful and fulfilling life.

Develop Growth Mindset

Looking back at my journey, I initially followed traditional thinking, concentrating on securing a job, which continued until my graduation. Following that, until around the age of forty, I passed through various struggles and explored different paths, encountering both challenges and successes. Subsequently, my focus shifted towards continuous skill development and developing a growth mindset. This stage was characterized by a conscious effort to acquire new skills, both personally and professionally. I actively sought opportunities for learning, whether through formal education, workshops, or practical experiences. The adoption of a growth mindset became pivotal during this time, developing a belief that abilities and intelligence can be developed with dedication and hard work. This mindset encouraged me to accept challenges as opportunities to learn and grow, leading to personal and professional development.

The concept of a growth mindset becomes a guiding individuals through challenges, setbacks, and the ever-evolving landscape of personal development. Instead of believing that our talents are fixed traits, a growth mindset teaches us that with dedication, hard work, and a thirst for knowledge, we can continually develop and evolve.

Let's break it down a bit further. Imagine a growth mindset as a superhero cape that empowers us to see challenges not as roadblocks but as stepping stones for growth. When faced with difficulties, those with a growth mindset don't shy away; instead, they roll up their sleeves and see it as an opportunity to learn and become even better. It's like looking at a puzzle and getting excited about figuring out how the pieces fit together.

This superhero cape becomes our constant companion. We approach the journey of managing ourselves with the understanding that our potential is not fixed. Setbacks aren't seen as failures; they're seen as plot twists that make the story more interesting.

Setting and pursuing goals become an art form with a growth mindset. Unlike fearing failure or avoiding challenges, individuals with this mindset eagerly set ambitious objectives. Why? Because they know that the journey itself is a significant contributor to personal growth. It's not just about reaching the destination; it's about the transformative process that happens along the way.

Now, let's discuss about how to use this superhero cape of a growth mindset in our self-management journey. First and foremost, it involves changing how we view challenges. Instead of seeing them as threats, we reframe them as opportunities for growth. It's like turning a daunting mountain into a thrilling climb. We accept the learning process, understanding that every experience, whether smooth or bumpy, contributes to our growth.

Seeking feedback becomes very useful too. Instead of fearing criticism, we welcome it as a valuable tool for improvement. It's like having a mentor guide us through the journey, pointing out areas where we can sharpen our skills. And here's the fun part – we celebrate efforts. It's not just about reaching the summit; it's about acknowledging the progress we make with every step.

Finally, adopting a growth mindset is a game-changer in self-management. It shapes our attitude, influences our actions, and turns the mundane into an exciting adventure. With this mindset, we steer life's twists and turns with optimism, resilience, and an unwavering commitment to becoming the best version of ourselves.

Build Good Habits

Building habits is like laying down the tracks for a smooth train journey towards effective self-management. Whether we realize it or not, habits are the silent architects of our daily lives, shaping the way we think, act, and ultimately live. The journey of intentional habit-building is a powerful strategy towards personal growth and achievement.

First and foremost, identifying areas that need attention or improvement is the launching pad for habit formation. It is like looking at a map and pinpointing the destinations we want to reach. For instance, if time management is challenging, creating a habit of prioritizing tasks and making a daily schedule becomes the compass. This habit of planning helps you solve the time management issue by giving you a clear direction for your day.

Consistency is the engine that propels the habit-building train forward. Research suggests that forming a new habit takes approximately 21 days, but the complexity of the behavior can influence this timeline. Think of it as laying down tracks; the more consistent the effort, the smoother the ride. During the initial stages, repetition and dedication are crucial. Setting realistic goals ensures that the journey remains manageable, preventing the overwhelm that might lead to derailment.

Now, let's talk about accountability and progress tracking – the conductors ensuring our habit-building train stays on course. Imagine sharing your habit goals with a friend or mentor; it's like having fellow passengers cheering you on throughout the journey. Additionally, using habit-tracking tools is like having a GPS system, providing real-time feedback on your progress. Regular assessments become the stops where you celebrate achievements, make necessary adjustments, and refuel your commitment to self-management.

The ultimate destination of habit-building for self-management is not just a point on the map; it's about creating a positive and sustainable lifestyle. These habits act as guiding stars, influencing your actions and decisions in alignment with your values and aspirations. Let's consider the example of a successful athlete. Their rigorous training routine, discipline in nutrition, and mental strength are not just sporadic efforts but intentional habits that propel them towards excellence. Similarly, successful individuals in any field often attribute their achievements to the intentional habits they have developed over time.

Building habits for self-management is not just about reaching a destination; it's about enjoying the journey. It's about empowering yourself to sail through life's twists and turns with resilience and purpose, developing a sense of fulfillment and well-being. So, let's continue on this habit-building journey, laying down tracks that lead to a more intentional, empowered, and fulfilling life.

Build Self-discipline

The degree of success one achieves is closely tied to the consistency of maintaining self-discipline throughout life. Greater commitment and steadfast adherence to self-discipline contribute to higher levels of success and fulfillment. Generally, individuals follow varying degrees of self-discipline in their lives. The more committed and consistent one is in practicing self-discipline, the better equipped they are to navigate challenges and attain greater success.

Self-discipline is the ability to regulate one's behavior, emotions, and impulses in harmony with overarching objectives. Imagine it as the conductor orchestrating the symphony of daily choices toward a harmonious and purposeful life. To embark on this transformative journey, individuals must begin with the foundational step of setting clear and achievable goals.

Goals act as inspirations, casting light on the path ahead. They need to be specific, measurable, and time-bound, functioning as a roadmap that guides actions. For instance, consider an aspiring writer aiming to complete a novel in six months. This specific goal not only provides direction but also becomes the driving force behind disciplined actions. The self-disciplined writer is less likely to succumb to procrastination or distractions, staying committed to the daily grind of writing.

Consistent habits form the building blocks of self-discipline. They infuse routine with purpose, ensuring that daily actions align with the desired destination. Take the example of a fitness enthusiast with a goal to run a marathon. Establishing a disciplined habit of daily running not only contributes to physical fitness but also instills a sense of commitment and perseverance. Over time, this habit becomes second nature, reinforcing the power of self-discipline in achieving long-term goals.

Developing a growth mindset is another facet of building self-discipline. This mindset, rooted in the belief that abilities can be developed through dedication and hard work, is a catalyst for resilience. Let's consider the journey of a successful entrepreneur who faced setbacks but accepted a growth mindset. Viewing failures as stepping stones, this entrepreneur persisted, adapted, and eventually achieved success. The growth mindset, intertwined with self-discipline, acted as a dynamic duo propelling them forward.

Developing self-discipline emerges as a crucial superpower, empowering individuals to steer through challenges, maintain focus on aspirations, and steadily progress toward their goals. Self-discipline guides towards positive actions, keeping them aligned with long-term objectives.

Building self-discipline is an ongoing process, demanding self-awareness, commitment, and a thirst for learning and adaptation. It is the thread weaving through the fabric of personal growth and resilience. As individuals embark on the quest to strengthen self-discipline, they not only enhance their ability to manage themselves effectively but also develop the resilience needed to thrive in the face of life's complexities.

Consider the journey of Serena Williams, an epitome of self-discipline in the world of sports. Despite facing numerous challenges and setbacks, Serena's steadfast commitment to her craft, rigorous training regimen, and focus on continuous improvement showcase the power of self-discipline. Her clear goal of becoming one of the greatest tennis players fueled disciplined habits, pushing her to consistently excel on the court.

Elon Musk, a visionary entrepreneur, is known for founding companies like Tesla and SpaceX. Musk's relentless pursuit of audacious goals, such as colonizing Mars, exemplifies the profound impact of self-discipline. His ability to set ambitious yet achievable goals, coupled with disciplined work habits and a growth mindset, has propelled him to the forefront of innovation.

These examples illustrate that building self-discipline is not a theoretical concept but a tangible force that shapes destinies. Whether in sports, entrepreneurship, or any other domain, individuals who master the art of self-discipline navigate challenges with resilience, maintain focus on their goals, and create a profound impact on the world around them.

Stress Management

Stress is an inevitable companion that can significantly impact our mental and physical well-being. Stress management, a key aspect of self-management, plays a pivotal role in facing life's challenges and achieving overall success. Let's go into the intricacies of stress management and its influence on different facets of an individual's life.

Maintaining Mental Health: Chronic stress is often associated with mental health issues, such as anxiety and depression. Imagine Naresh, a young professional juggling a demanding job and family responsibilities. The constant pressure led to heightened stress, impacting his mental health. Through adopting stress management techniques like mindfulness and deep breathing exercises, Naresh learned to cope with stressors effectively. This not only eased his anxiety but also improved his overall mental well-being, enabling his to approach life with a more positive outlook.

Preserving Physical Health: The toll of stress extends beyond the mind, affecting physical health. Tarun, a student was preparing for crucial exams. The stress of academic expectations started affecting his sleep and digestion. To get rid of this issue, Tarun incorporated regular exercise and a balanced diet into his routine. These practices not only helped in alleviating stress-related physical symptoms but also contributed to a healthier lifestyle, showcasing the intricate link between stress management and physical well-being.

Enhancing Productivity: Stress management is a catalyst for increased productivity. Harish, a professional dealing with tight deadlines, noticed that unmanaged stress hindered his focus and decision-making abilities. By integrating stress reduction techniques such as time management and short breaks, Harish experienced a boost in productivity. Stress management became his secret weapon, enabling him to perform optimally in both personal and professional spheres.

Building Resilience: Life is full of challenges, and the ability to manage stress is synonymous with resilience. Gagan, an entrepreneur facing uncertainties in his business. By implementing resilience-building strategies like accepting change and maintaining a positive mindset, Gagan turned stressors into opportunities for growth. Stress management became his tool for navigating through the complexities of entrepreneurship with adaptability and grace.

Developing Healthy Relationships: Unmanaged stress can strain relationships. Tom, was working in a high-stakes job, found that stress was affecting his interactions with family and friends. By incorporating stress management practices such as effective communication and setting boundaries, Tom learned to maintain healthier relationships. Stress management became an essential component of his self-management journey, contributing to a more balanced and fulfilling social life.

Stress management is not just a coping mechanism. It's a fundamental aspect of effective self-management. Through real-life examples, we see how individuals can transform their lives by incorporating stress management practices. From mental and physical well-being to productivity, resilience, and healthy relationships, the impact of stress management resonates across various dimensions, empowering individuals to lead more balanced and fulfilling lives.

Time Management

The way we manage our time becomes the choreography that shapes our journey. Imagine time as a precious currency, and time management as the art of investing wisely. It's not about managing time itself, for time flows relentlessly; it's about managing ourselves within its current. Let's uncover the significance of time management, understanding why it's the roadmap to success in effective self-management.

Prioritization of Tasks: Imagine a juggler skillfully tossing multiple balls in the air. Each ball represents a task or responsibility. Effective time management allows us to prioritize these tasks based on their significance and urgency. It's about recognizing which balls are made of glass (crucial tasks) and need our utmost attention, and which are made of rubber (less critical tasks) and can bounce back if momentarily dropped.

Increased Productivity: Have you ever noticed how a focused sprint yields better results than a scattered marathon? Time management is the architect behind this productivity magic. By dedicating specific time slots to tasks, we create an environment where our attention isn't divided. This focused approach to work not only enhances productivity but also elevates the quality of our output.

Reduced Stress and Overwhelm: Imagine navigating a chaotic maze without a map. This is akin to navigating life without effective time management. Chaos breeds stress, and stress begets overwhelm. Breaking down larger tasks into smaller, manageable steps and setting realistic deadlines acts as our compass, guiding us through the maze with a sense of purpose and direction.

Goal Achievement: Goals are the destinations we set for ourselves. Effective time management is the roadmap that guides us toward these destinations. It's about charting the course, marking milestones, and ensuring steady progress. Without this roadmap, goals remain mere aspirations, and the journey becomes aimless.

Improved Decision-Making: Have you ever made a hasty decision when pressed for time? In the absence of thoughtful time management, decisions often become hurried, leading to mistakes. A well-organized schedule provides the luxury of time and mental clarity, allowing us to make informed decisions rather than impulsive ones.

Work-Life Balance: The delicate equilibrium between work, personal life, and leisure is a tightrope walk. Effective time management ensures that we allocate time not just for professional commitments but also for self-care, relaxation, and the pursuit of hobbies. It's about harmonizing the various facets of life to create a symphony of well-being.

Enhanced Focus and Concentration: In a world of constant distractions, focus is a superpower. Time management creates the environment for this superpower to thrive. By breaking the day into dedicated time blocks for specific tasks, we eliminate the need for multitasking. This, in turn, enhances focus, concentration, and the overall quality of our work.

Adaptability to Changes: Life is unpredictable. Unforeseen circumstances can disrupt even the most meticulously crafted plans. Effective time management, however, instills a sense of flexibility and adaptability. It's the ability to navigate diversions without losing sight of the destination, minimizing disruptions and maintaining control.

Increased Accountability: Imagine setting sail without a compass or a destination. Time management is our compass, and setting clear deadlines and timeframes is akin to plotting our course. This accountability to deadlines develops a sense of responsibility and commitment to achieving our set objectives.

Optimized Use of Resources: Time, like any valuable resource, should be used judiciously. Effective time management ensures the optimized use of this resource. It's about minimizing the time spent on unproductive activities and maximizing the return on investment in each moment.

To summarize, time management is not about controlling time; it's about mastering ourselves within its rhythmic flow. As we follow the art of managing ourselves effectively within the confines of time, we unlock the doors to personal and professional success. It's the magic wand that transforms chaos into order, stress into serenity, and aspirations into achievements. The journey of self-management begins with a conscious effort to navigate time's currents with purpose, ensuring a well-balanced and fulfilling life.

Emotional Intelligence

Emotional intelligence, a key component of self-management, plays a key role in how individuals understand, regulate, and express their emotions. It involves recognizing and comprehending one's own feelings, effectively managing them, and using emotional information to guide behavior. Here's how emotional intelligence is crucial for effective self-management:

Self-awareness: Emotional intelligence begins with self-awareness – the ability to recognize and understand one's own emotions. Individuals with high EI are attuned to their feelings, identifying not only the surface-level emotions but also the underlying causes and triggers. This self-awareness forms the foundation for effective self-management.

Emotional regulation: A significant aspect of self-management is the ability to regulate emotions appropriately. This involves controlling impulsive reactions, managing stress, and adapting to changing situations. High emotional intelligence enables individuals to navigate challenging emotions, preventing them from overwhelming decision-making and behavior.

Motivation: Motivation is a key factor in self-management, and emotional intelligence contributes by enhancing intrinsic motivation. Individuals with high EI are often driven by a strong sense of purpose, using their emotions as a source of energy and commitment. This internal motivation helps in staying focused on long-term goals and overcoming obstacles.

Effective communication: Emotional intelligence plays a vital role in interpersonal relationships, and effective communication is a part of self-management. Understanding one's emotions allows for clearer expression, active listening, and empathetic communication. This, in turn, develops better collaboration and relationship management.

Resilience: Resilience, the ability to bounce back from setbacks, is a crucial aspect of self-management. Emotionally intelligent individuals can cope with adversity more effectively, learning from failures, and maintaining a positive outlook. Their ability to regulate emotions enables them to navigate challenges without being overwhelmed.

Conflict resolution: Dealing with conflicts is an inevitable part of life, and emotional intelligence aids in navigating these situations. By understanding and managing one's emotions, individuals can approach conflicts with a calm and rational mindset. This helps in finding constructive solutions and maintaining positive relationships.

Decision-making: Emotions play a significant role in decision-making. Individuals with high emotional intelligence can assess situations holistically, considering both rational and emotional aspects. This balanced approach leads to more informed and thoughtful decision-making, aligning with long-term goals and personal values.

In essence, emotional intelligence is a cornerstone of effective self-management. It empowers individuals to navigate their emotions, make informed decisions, build strong relationships, and develop resilience in the face of life's challenges. Developing emotional intelligence is a continuous process that enhances overall well-being and personal growth.

Decision Making

Making decisions is a fundamental element of self-management, playing a crucial role in shaping an individual's life and overall well-being. The choices individuals make on a daily basis influence their personal and professional paths, impacting their relationships, health, and overall happiness. Here are several ways in which decision-making is essential in self-management:

Defining Priorities: Effective decision-making helps individuals clarify their priorities. By understanding what matters most to them, individuals can align their choices with their values and long-term goals. This clarity guides actions and ensures that time and energy are invested in areas that contribute to personal fulfillment.

Setting Goals: Decision-making is integral to setting and achieving goals. Whether it's outlining career objectives, health targets, or personal milestones, the choices made in daily life contribute to progress. Thoughtful decision-making involves considering the implications of each choice on long-term aspirations.

Problem Solving: Life is filled with challenges and uncertainties. Effective decision-making involves a problem-solving mindset, enabling individuals to analyze situations, identify potential solutions, and choose the most appropriate course of action. This skill is crucial for navigating obstacles and overcoming setbacks.

Time Management: Decision-making is closely linked to time management. Choosing how to allocate time among various tasks and responsibilities requires evaluating priorities and making decisions that optimize productivity and well-being. Wise decisions about time usage contribute to reduced stress and increased efficiency.

Emotional Regulation: Decision-making is influenced by emotions, and in turn, decisions impact emotional well-being. Developing emotional intelligence allows individuals to make decisions with a balanced perspective, considering both rational and emotional aspects. This ability develops resilience and helps manage stress effectively.

Personal Development: Decision-making is intertwined with personal development. Each choice made contributes to learning and growth. Accepting decisions as learning opportunities, even when mistakes occur, enhances self-awareness and resilience. Reflecting on decisions facilitates continuous improvement and adaptability.

Cultivating Autonomy: Self-management involves cultivating autonomy and taking responsibility for one's life. Decision-making is the cornerstone of autonomy, allowing individuals to assert control over their choices and actions. This sense of agency contributes to a greater sense of self-efficacy.

Decision-making is the compass that guides individuals on their journey of self-management. From daily choices to significant life-altering decisions, each one shapes the narrative of one's life. Developing the skill of thoughtful decision-making empowers individuals to lead purposeful, fulfilling lives aligned with their values and aspirations.

Continuous Learning

Continuous learning emerges as a powerful force, shaping the way we manage ourselves and navigate the complexities that unfold. It serves as a guiding light, contributing significantly to personal growth, adaptability, and overall well-being. Imagine it as a lifelong adventure, where each piece of knowledge becomes a stepping stone toward a more enriched and fulfilled existence.

In our rapidly changing world, marked by technological advancements, the importance of continuous learning cannot be overstated. It's the secret sauce that keeps us relevant, agile, and ready to face the challenges that come our way. For instance, the ever-evolving workplace, embracing new skills and staying abreast of industry trends isn't just beneficial; it's a necessity. Those who embody a mindset of continuous learning find themselves equipped to navigate change with confidence, standing resilient in the face of life's uncertainties.

Elon Musk's insatiable appetite for learning is evident in his diverse ventures. From creating ground-breaking electric vehicles to exploring the realms of space travel, Musk's commitment to continuous learning has been a driving force behind his ability to lead transformative endeavors.

Continuous learning is not just a tool for adapting to change; it's a catalyst for enhanced problem-solving skills. When we expose ourselves to diverse perspectives and willingly explore new set of information, we nurture a creative and versatile approach to overcoming challenges. This adaptive thinking is the cornerstone of effective self-management, empowering individuals to not only tackle obstacles but to do so with ingenuity and resourcefulness.

Moreover, the journey of continuous learning is intrinsically tied to personal development and a sense of accomplishment. Imagine setting a goal to acquire a new skill or delve into a subject previously unexplored. As you follow the path of learning, each milestone achieved, no matter how small, contributes to a positive self-image and a heightened sense of purpose. The pursuit of knowledge becomes a dynamic journey of self-discovery, unlocking untapped potential and allowing individuals to redefine their aspirations continually.

Let's go deep into the concept of emotional intelligence, another realm where continuous learning plays a transformative role. As we expose ourselves to different perspectives and accumulate experiences, our emotional intelligence is refined. This heightened awareness and understanding of our own emotions, coupled with the ability to navigate interpersonal relationships adeptly, become invaluable assets in maintaining overall well-being.

In short, continuous learning is the heartbeat of effective self-management. It is the force that equips individuals with the skills and mindset needed to not only adapt to change but to accept it with open arms. It enhances problem-solving abilities, develops personal development, and contributes to improved emotional intelligence. By making a commitment to lifelong learning, individuals embark on a journey marked by resilience, purpose, and an unending thirst for knowledge.

So, as we navigate the ebb and flow of life, let continuous learning be our compass, guiding us toward a future where we manage ourselves not just capably but with a spirit of curiosity, growth, and perpetual learning. After all, in a world that continually evolves, the ability to learn, unlearn, and relearn is the true essence of effective self-management.

Communication Skills

Communication skills serve as the bedrock of effective self-management, weaving through the fabric of expressing needs, setting boundaries, and forging meaningful connections. At the heart of self-management communication lies the art of self-talk – the internal dialogue that shapes thoughts, emotions, and actions. Imagine, Positive self-talk is like a personal cheerleader, boosting resilience and confidence. On the flip side, negative self-talk can cast shadows of stress and self-doubt. It's akin to having a supportive friend within, nudging you toward optimism and encouragement.

Rancho, a young professional, faces the challenges of a new job. His positive self-talk serves as a constant motivator, helping his navigate setbacks with a can-do attitude. On the contrary, Mark, grappling with self-doubt, finds his negative self-talk acting as a roadblock to his professional growth. Here, you can understand the power of self-talk in self-management.

Clear communication is the key to healthy connections. Imagine Kabir articulating his expectations to his roommate, ensuring a harmonious living environment. In contrast, Kaye, struggling to express her desires, finds her relationships strained. The ability to communicate needs and desires in relationships is fundamental to effective self-management.

Now, let's dive into conflict resolution. Envision a workplace where team members communicate openly, actively listen, and negotiate compromises. In this realm, conflicts are not roadblocks but opportunities for growth. Imagine Grishma, adept at articulating her thoughts assertively during team discussions, contributing to a collaborative work environment. On the flip side, Jacob, hesitant to express his concerns, experiences heightened stress. Here, communication skills become the sword and shield in the battle of conflicts.

Beyond conflict, effective communication serves as a lifeline for seeking support and building a robust network. Imagine Tim, facing a personal challenge, reaching out to friends and family with clarity and openness. His ability to communicate authentically creates a safety net that bolsters his emotional well-being. Contrast this with Emily, hesitant to express her struggles, who finds herself isolated during tough times. Communication, in this context, becomes the bridge that connects individuals with the resources, guidance, and encouragement necessary for effective self-management.

To summarize, communication skills are the dynamic force steering the ship of self-management. Whether it's the internal dialogue shaping thoughts or the external expression of needs and boundaries, mastering communication is the compass guiding individuals to enhanced well-being. As individuals sharpen these skills, they unlock the door to a more fulfilling and well-managed life, filled with positive connections and effective conflict resolution.

Adaptability

Adaptability acts as a secret weapon that equips individuals to dance through the unpredictable twists and turns of life. Imagine life as a thrilling rollercoaster, with adaptability as your trusty safety harness, ensuring you not only survive but thrive in the face of challenges. Let's unravel the magic behind adaptability, exploring its various facets that transform ordinary individuals into superheroes of their own stories.

Flexibility in Thinking: Think of adaptability as a mental gymnast, effortlessly performing flips and twists in the face of changing circumstances. Imagine you're planning a picnic, and the weather decides to play a prank on your sunny day. Someone with high adaptability doesn't crumble in disappointment but swiftly transforms the picnic plan into a cozy indoor game night. Flexibility in thinking involves following diverse perspectives and exploring alternative solutions, turning unexpected challenges into opportunities for creativity and innovation.

Emotional Resilience: Life is like a rollercoaster, and sometimes it throws unexpected loop-de-loops your way. Now, imagine you're learning to ride a bike, and every time you stumble, you not only get back up but also learn to do a cool trick. That's emotional resilience—the ability to bounce back from challenges, maintain composure when things go haywire, and turn setbacks into valuable lessons. Emotionally resilient individuals ride the waves of life with a surfboard of positivity, emerging stronger and wiser after each storm.

A Willingness to Learn and Grow: In a rapidly changing world where the only constant is change itself, adaptability is your superpower for staying relevant and competitive. It's akin to being a skilled gardener who not only tends to the existing plants but also eagerly plants new seeds, anticipating a future lush with possibilities. A commitment to learning is the key, allowing individuals to acquire new skills, stay updated on emerging trends, and develop a mindset of continuous improvement.

Effective Interpersonal Relationships: Think about a vibrant social gathering as a bustling marketplace, each person bringing their unique stall of ideas, perspectives, and communication styles. Adaptable individuals are like social chameleons, effortlessly navigating this bustling marketplace. They understand the art of connecting with different personalities, collaborating effectively, and resolving conflicts with finesse. In the grand dance of social interactions, adaptability becomes the melody that harmonizes diverse notes into a beautiful symphony.

In simple terms, being adaptable is like wearing a superhero cape that transforms regular people into the heroes of their own adventures. It's not just about getting through life; it's about thriving in its ever-changing excitement. Whether it's looking at things from different angles, bouncing back from tough times, gaining new knowledge, or gracefully navigating social situations, adaptability lets individuals not only deal with change but welcome it with curiosity, strength, and growth. So, put on your adaptability cape because the rollercoaster of life is here, and you're the superhero skillfully handling its twists and turns!Top of Form

Accountability

Accepting accountability is like stepping into the driver's seat of your life, holding the steering wheel of personal growth and confidence. You might wonder why some individuals shy away from responsibility. Well, it's often because they're uncertain about what might happen or the challenges they might face. But, accountability is not a burden; it's highly beneficial for positive change.

Imagine your life is a movie, and you're the main character. Now, when you take responsibility for your actions, decisions, and how things turn out, you become the hero of your story. It's not just about going with the flow; it's about actively shaping your destiny. Imagine it like upgrading from being a spectator to the director of your life movie. That's the kind of mindset that turns fear into power and makes you resilient.

Taking accountability is like becoming the captain of your ship. You're not just sailing along; you're steering towards your destination. It means recognizing your role in both successes and setbacks. Think of it as owning the script of your life. This self-awareness is like having your own treasure map, leading to increased self-esteem and confidence.

In simpler terms, personal growth is like a video game, and accountability is your controller. You navigate through challenges, collecting power-ups and gaining points. It's a courageous step that transforms fear into a boost for personal growth. Picture it as opening doors to new levels of opportunities and challenges. As you navigate life with responsibility, you not only level up personally but also contribute positively to the world around you.

Now, let's dive into self-management. It's like being the CEO of your life, making sure everything runs smoothly. Setting goals is a crucial part of this. Imagine each goal as a quest in your favorite video game. Being accountable to yourself ensures you're on track, making progress, and winning achievements. It's like having cheat codes for a purpose-driven journey.

Discipline and resilience are your superpowers in this game of life. Knowing you are responsible for your choices encourages positive habits. Whether it's maintaining a healthy lifestyle or working towards career goals, being accountable establishes a sense of ownership and commitment. It's like having a gym buddy, but for all aspects of your life.

Now, think of accountability as your personal coach. Regularly checking in on your progress allows for self-assessment and adjustments. It's like having a halftime review during a sports match. You analyze what's working, what needs improvement, and strategize for the next half. This constant feedback loop ensures continuous improvement, making you adaptable and self-aware.

Without accountability, self-management can feel like a ship without a captain. Procrastination and a lack of focus might take over. On the other hand, embracing accountability puts you in the driver's seat. It's like having a GPS guiding you through obstacles, helping you learn from failures, and persistently moving towards your objectives. So, embrace accountability, level up in the game of personal growth, and make your life's story an epic adventure.

Sense of Purpose

Discovering your sense of purpose is like finding the North Star in the vast sky of life. It's not just about achieving things or getting praise from others; it's about understanding why you do what you do and what truly matters to you. Think of a sense of purpose as your personal cheerleader, especially when faced with tough times. It's like having a powerful engine inside you that propels you forward, turning obstacles into stepping stones for growth. Instead of seeing challenges as roadblocks, you see them as opportunities to become a better version of yourself. That's the magic of having a clear sense of purpose – it keeps you moving forward with determination and resilience.

Now, let's talk about decision-making. Life is full of choices, and having a sense of purpose helps in making decisions. When you're unsure about what to do, you can turn to your sense of purpose as a guide. It helps you make choices that align with your values and long-term dreams, steering you away from distractions or short-term gains that might not bring you real happiness.

Finding your sense of purpose isn't a one-time thing; it's a journey of self-discovery. It involves looking within yourself, understanding what you value, what makes you passionate, and how you want to make a positive impact on the world. Maybe it's about contributing to a cause, building meaningful relationships, or growing as an individual. Whatever it is, your sense of purpose evolves as you grow and experience different parts of life.

A sense of purpose is like a lighthouse, guiding you through the waves of life toward meaningful destinations. When it comes to self-management, it gives you the strength to face challenges, make decisions that resonate with your core values, and lead a life that feels true to who you are. Developing your sense of purpose isn't just a journey of self-discovery; it's a transformative experience that shapes not only how you manage yourself but also the positive impact you can have on the world around you.

Motivation

Motivation is the kickstart that gets you moving, the force that keeps you going, and the cheerleader that celebrates your victories, big or small. Let's take a closer look at why motivation is your trusty companion on this journey of self-management.

Imagine motivation as the fuel that powers your self-improvement engine. It's the magic that turns vague ideas into concrete goals. When you're motivated, you start envisioning a better version of yourself. Whether it's acing that project at work, running a marathon, or simply leading a healthier lifestyle, motivation is what sets the wheels in motion.

Suppose, motivation is your personal coach, standing by your side during the inevitable hurdles of life. Self-management isn't a walk in the park; it's a journey with its fair share of challenges. Here's where motivation steps in as your resilience booster. When setbacks happen, and doubts creep in, motivation becomes the voice in your head saying, "You've got this." It's the force that keeps you going when the going gets tough.

But motivation isn't just about getting started or pushing through challenges; it's also your guide in your daily life. Life is busy, and distractions are everywhere. Motivation acts as your internal GPS, helping you stay on course. It keeps your eyes on the prize, making sure you don't lose sight of your goals amid the noise of daily life. With motivation as your guide, you can manage your time wisely, prioritize effectively, and make choices that align with your bigger picture.

Motivation is the architect behind positive habits. Whether you're trying to eat healthier, learn a new skill, or enhance your emotional well-being, motivation is what nudges you to take that first step. It transforms routine tasks into purposeful actions, making every small effort feel like a win. Motivation turns self-improvement into a journey filled with fulfillment and accomplishment.

Therefore, motivation is your wingman in self-management. It's the spark that lights the fire of progress. Understanding its role is like unlocking a superpower—one that helps you set goals, overcome obstacles, stay focused, and build positive habits. So, as you embark on your journey of self-management, let motivation be your trusted companion, cheering you on every step of the way.

Resilience

Resilience helps you bounce back when life throws curveballs your way. It's a crucial skill in self-management, which means being the boss of your own life. Let's dive into why resilience is so important.

First off, resilience helps you adapt. Imagine you're playing your favorite video game, and suddenly the rules change. Resilience is what lets you figure out the new rules, find new strategies, and keep playing without getting frustrated. Life is a bit like that – full of surprises and changes. Resilience is your secret weapon to handle all those twists and turns.

Now, let's talk about emotions. Have you ever felt really angry or sad about something? Resilience is like having a shield for your feelings. Instead of letting negative emotions take over, resilient people can process those feelings in a healthy way. It's like being a superhero who knows how to handle their emotions, so they don't take over and make everything messy.

Life can be stressful, right? Resilience is your sidekick in managing stress. It's like having a cool strategy for every stressful level in the game of life. Resilience keeps you from burning out and helps you stay chill even when things get tough.

Now, imagine you're working really hard on a big project, like building the tallest tower. Suddenly, your tower collapses! Resilience is what helps you keep your focus. Instead of giving up, you look at the fallen blocks, think of a new plan, and start building again. In life, resilience helps you stay focused on your goals, even when things don't go as planned.

Having a positive mindset is like having a treasure map to find the good stuff in life. Resilience is your guide to that treasure. When something goes wrong, resilient people see it as a challenge, not a disaster. It's like being an explorer who finds hidden gems in every part of the journey. This positive outlook makes life more fun and exciting.

Now, let's talk about confidence. Imagine you're learning to ride a bycycle, and you fall off a few times. Resilience is what helps you get back on and try again. Each time you try, you become more confident in your ability to ride. In life, every challenge you overcome with resilience builds your confidence. It's like gaining experience points in a game, making you stronger and more capable.

Lastly, resilience is your secret weapon for making good decisions. Life often puts you in situations where you have to make choices – like deciding which path to take in a maze. Resilience helps you make clear decisions without being too influenced by stress or mistakes. It's like having a wise guide to help you choose the best path.

Resilience helps you handle whatever comes your way – from changes and challenges to emotions and stress. By being adaptable, emotionally strong, and positive, resilience becomes your trusted companion in achieving your goals and keeping your life on track.

Conclusion

The art of self-management is not a destination but a continuous, enriching journey that extends throughout our lives. It is a commitment to understanding ourselves, embracing personal growth, and navigating the complexities of life with resilience and purpose. As we tread this path, we unearth the power within to shape our destiny, overcome challenges, and savor the moments of triumph.

Self-management is not about achieving perfection but about striving for progress, learning from experiences, and cultivating resilience. It is an ongoing process of self-discovery, where we harness our strengths, acknowledge our vulnerabilities, and consistently work towards becoming the best version of ourselves. This journey is an invitation to transform setbacks into stepping stones, failures into lessons, and moments of despair into opportunities for growth.

Self-management empowers us to adapt to change, make informed decisions, and develop a sense of balance amidst chaos. It is a commitment to our well-being, recognizing that a holistic and harmonious life encompasses not only professional achievements but also personal contentment, emotional resilience, and meaningful connections.

So, let us follow the lifelong voyage of self-management with open hearts and determined spirits. May we find joy in the process, wisdom in the lessons, and fulfillment in the continuous pursuit of becoming the architects of our destinies. The art of self-management is not confined to a particular phase; it is a companion for the entire journey, guiding us towards a life of purpose, resilience, and enduring satisfaction.

Self-Management Checklist

This checklist serves as a comprehensive guide to help you develop essential skills and habits for personal and professional success. Self-management is the cornerstone of achieving your goals, developing resilience, and leading a fulfilling life. By following this checklist, you will embark on a journey of self-discovery, growth, and empowerment.

Each point on this checklist represents a key aspect of self-management, ranging from goal setting and time management to resilience and communication skills. By integrating these practices into your daily life, you will develop the ability to navigate challenges, make informed decisions, and maintain a healthy work-life balance. Moreover, you will develop a sense of purpose, integrity, and values that guide your actions and interactions with others.

Whether you are a student, professional, or entrepreneur, this checklist is designed to help you harness your potential and thrive in all aspects of your life. Take the time to reflect on each point, identify areas for improvement, and commit to making positive changes.

Self-management is not about perfection but progress. So, enjoy the journey, celebrate your successes, and learn from setbacks as you strive to become the best version of yourself.

- Set Clear Goals: Define your short-term and long-term objectives in alignment with your purpose and values, ensuring they are specific, measurable, achievable, relevant, and time-bound (SMART).
- Prioritize Tasks: Identify your most important tasks and prioritize them based on urgency, importance, and alignment with your values.
- Time Management: Allocate your time effectively, using techniques such as time blocking, Pomodoro technique, or Eisenhower matrix, while ensuring activities align with your purpose.

- Create Daily Rituals: Establish productive daily rituals that support your goals, purpose, and values, such as morning routines, exercise habits, or reflection practices.
- Develop Self-Discipline: Develop self-discipline rooted in your values and integrity to stay focused, motivated, and consistent in pursuing your goals, even in the face of challenges.
- Manage Stress: Implement stress management techniques, such as deep breathing, mindfulness, or physical exercise, to reduce stress and maintain resilience while staying true to your values.
- Enhance Productivity: Adopt productivity tools and strategies that honor your values and integrity, such as to-do lists, productivity apps, or task delegation, to maximize your efficiency.
- Improve Decision-Making: Enhance your decision-making skills by considering your

purpose, values, and long-term consequences, and aligning choices with integrity.

- Develop Self-Awareness: Practice self-reflection and self-awareness to understand your purpose, values, strengths, weaknesses, and emotions, guiding your actions and decisions.
- Build Resilience: Develop resilience rooted in your purpose and values to bounce back from setbacks, learn from failures, and adapt to changes with integrity and a growth mindset.
- Develop Growth Mindset: Develop a growth mindset aligned with your purpose and values, viewing challenges as opportunities for learning and growth, developing continuous improvement.
- Manage Energy Levels: Monitor and manage your energy levels throughout the day by prioritizing tasks according to your purpose, values, and peak performance times.

- Maintain Work-Life Balance: Strive to achieve a healthy balance between work, personal life, relationships, and self-care activities while honoring your purpose and values.
- Seek Feedback: Solicit feedback from others to gain valuable insights into your performance, behavior, and alignment with your purpose, values, and integrity.
- Develop Communication Skills: Enhance your communication skills, including listening, speaking, writing, and nonverbal communication, to build strong relationships and convey your values and integrity effectively.
- Practice Empathy: Develop empathy rooted in your values to understand and connect with others' perspectives, emotions, and experiences, developing meaningful relationships with integrity.
- Set Boundaries: Establish clear boundaries aligned with your purpose, values, and integrity to protect your time, energy, and

well-being, and communicate them assertively to others.

- Accept Change: Accept change as a natural part of life, aligning your actions and decisions with your purpose, values, and integrity while adapting to new circumstances with flexibility and openness.
- Learn Continuously: Commit to lifelong learning and personal development aligned with your purpose, values, and integrity by pursuig formal education, attending workshops, reading books, or seeking mentorship.
- Manage Finances: Take control of your finances by budgeting, saving, investing wisely, and planning for future financial security in alignment with your purpose, values, and integrity.
- Nurture Relationships: Invest time and effort in building and nurturing meaningful relationships with family,

friends, colleagues, and mentors while honoring your values and integrity.
- Practice Gratitude: Develop a mindset of gratitude aligned with your purpose and values by appreciating the positive aspects of your life, expressing thanks, and focusing on abundance with integrity.
- Take Ownership: Take ownership of your actions, decisions, and outcomes, and avoid blaming others or making excuses, demonstrating integrity and accountability.
- Stay Organized: Maintain an organized environment, both physically and digitally, to reduce clutter, increase productivity, and reduce stress, reflecting your purpose, values, and integrity.
- Reflect and Adjust: Regularly reflect on your progress, achievements, and challenges, and adjust your strategies and behaviors accordingly to stay aligned with your purpose, values, and integrity while

striving for personal and professional success.

<u>Join My Community</u>

https://community.askpndas.com/

www.ingramcontent.com/pod-product-compliance
Lightning Source LLC
Chambersburg PA
CBHW070352230526
45471CB00006B/2530